Follow the directions below.

1. Color the clown's hair orange.
2. Color his hat purple.
3. Color his shoes brown and his dog black.
   4. Color the squares on his clothes green, the circles blue, and the triangles purple.

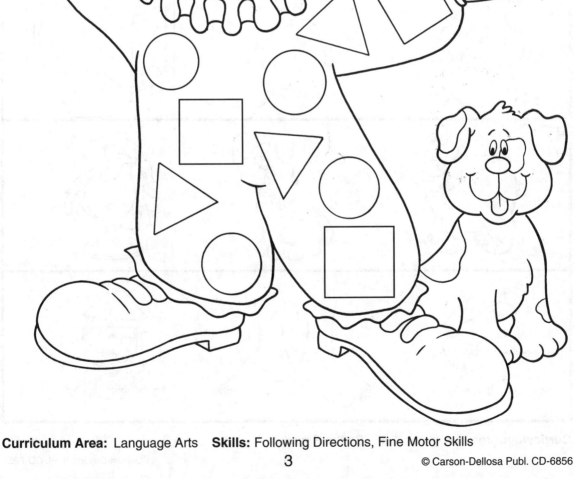

Curriculum Area: Language Arts   **Skills:** Following Directions, Fine Motor Skills

3

Circle the two pictures in each row that **rhyme**.

Curriculum Area: Language Arts **Skills:** Rhyming

© Carson-Dellosa Publ. CD-6856

Circle the two pictures in each row that begin with the **same sound**.

Curriculum Area: Language Arts **Skills:** Discriminating Between Sounds, Recognizing Objects

Look at the pictures. Write the letter you hear at the **end** of each word.

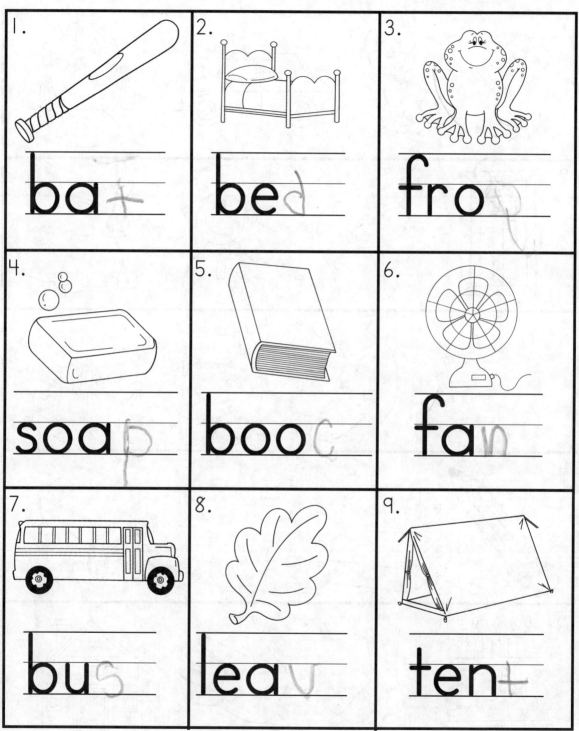

1. ba**t**

2. be**d**

3. fro**g**

4. soa**p**

5. boo**c**

6. fa**n**

7. bu**s**

8. lea**v**

9. ten**t**

Number the pictures in each row **1, 2,** or **3** to show the correct order.

Curriculum Area: Language Arts   **Skills:** Sequencing

7

© Carson-Dellosa Publ. CD-6856

Circle the picture in each row that **does not belong** with the others.

© Carson-Dellosa Publ. CD-6856

For each box, fill in the circle next to the word that **matches** the picture.

1. O sock O shoe O star	2. O car O cow O can	3. O house O chin O chair
4. O stop O star O coat	5. O flower O flag O fan	6. O clock O cat O clown
7. O door O drum O sun	8. O wing O wish O fish	9. O map O mop O man

Circle the word that goes with each picture.

1. bee   bees

2. box   boxes

3. sock   socks

4. fly   flies

5. baby   babies

6. bus   buses

7. car   cars

8. glass   glasses

9. mouse   mice

10. star   stars

11. squirrel   squirrels

12. dish   dishes

Curriculum Area: Language Arts   **Skills:** Matching, Recognizing Singular and Plural Words

Write the title of your favorite story. Draw pictures to show what happened at the beginning, the middle, and the end of the story.

Title: _____

_____

_____

beginning

middle

end

Curriculum Area: Language Arts **Skills:** Recalling Facts, Illustrating Thoughts

Look at the picture of the book, then finish the sentences below.

1. The author of the book is

_____

_____

_____ •

2. The title of the book is

_____

_____

_____ •

3. The illustrator of the book is

_____

_____

_____ •

Draw a line from each word in the left column to its **opposite** in the right column.

up

dry

first

on

left

happy

yes

big

last

down

right

wet

off

no

little

sad

Draw a line from each word in the left column to a word that means about the **same** thing in the right column.

friend	above
kind	pal
over	nice
wise	tiny
little	smart
happy	chilly
big	large
cold	glad

Think of a book you like to read. Draw the character you like best in the story, then finish the sentences below.

My favorite character's name is

_____

_____

_____

I like this character best because

_____

_____

_____

_____

_____

_____

Curriculum Area: Language Arts   **Skills:** Illustrating Thoughts, Composing Sentences

Write the words in **alphabetical order**.

1.

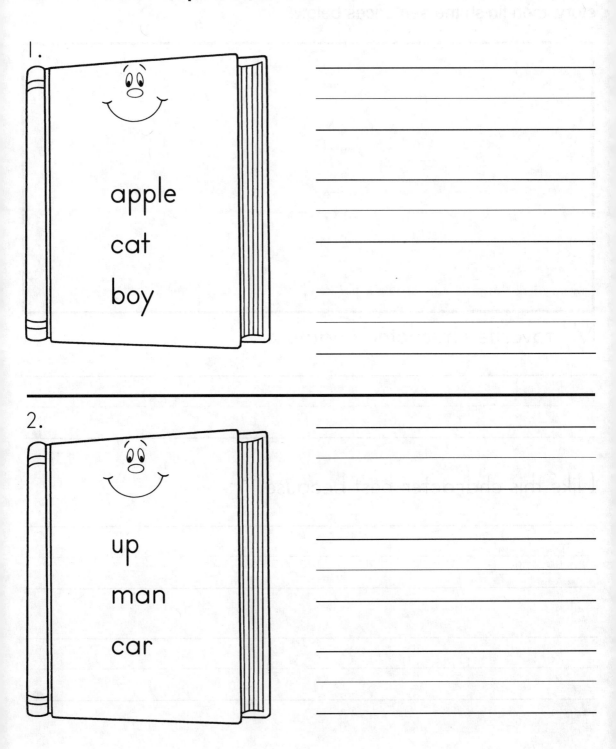

apple
cat
boy

_____
_____
_____
_____
_____
_____
_____
_____

2.

up
man
car

_____
_____
_____
_____
_____
_____
_____
_____

Curriculum Area: Language Arts   **Skills:** Alphabetizing, Writing

Fill in the missing **days**. Draw a line from each day to its **abbreviation**.

Sunday   Tues.

_____
_____   Sun.

_____
_____   Mon.
_____

Wednesday   Sat.

Thursday
                                          Thurs.

_____
_____

                                          Wed.
_____
_____

_____   Fri.

Write in the missing **months**.

January

February

March

April

_____

_____

_____

_____

_____

_____

July

_____

_____

September

October

November

December

January					
1	2	3	4	5	6
7	8	9	10	11	12	13
14	15	16	17	18	19	20
21	22	23	24	25	26	27
28	29	30	31		

May					
		1	2	3	4
5	6	7	8	9	10	11
12	13	14	15	16	17	18
19	20	21	22	23	24	25
	27	28	29	30	31

December					
1	2	3	4	5	6	7
8	9	10	11	12	13	14
15	16	17	18	19	20	21
22	23	24	25	26	27	28
29	30	31			

Curriculum Area: Language Arts   **Skills:** Sequencing Months of the Year

18

A **sentence** is a group of words that expresses a complete thought. A sentence begins with a capital letter.

Unscramble each group of words and make a sentence.

1. dog   See   run.   the

_____

_____

_____

2. like   play   ball.   I   to

_____

_____

_____

3. day.   is   It   a   cloudy

_____

_____

_____

4. friend   My   Eve.   is   named

_____

_____

_____

A **telling sentence** ends with a period. (.)
An **asking sentence** ends with a question mark. (?)

Circle the correct punctuation mark for each sentence.

1. We went to a farm . ?

2. We rode on a bus . ?

3. Have you ever been to a farm . ?

4. We saw some cows . ?

5. We got to milk the cow . ?

6. Did you ever milk a cow . ?

7. Would you like to have a pig . ?

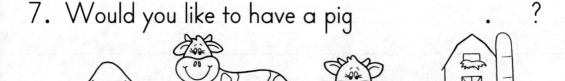

For each box, circle the picture that goes with the sentence.

The bee is on the flower.

The boy has a bat.

The lion is in the cage.

The frogs like to jump.

Curriculum Area: Language Arts   **Skills:** Visual Discrimination, Reading Comprehension

Write the missing vowel: **a, e, i, o,** or **u.**

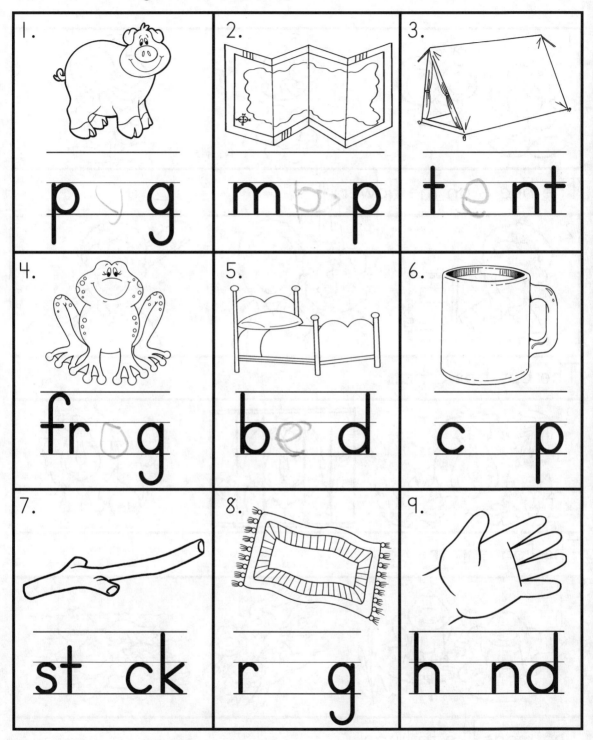

1. p _ g

2. m _ p

3. t e n t

4. f r _ g

5. b e d

6. c _ p

7. s t _ c k

8. r _ g

9. h _ n d

Write the missing blend: **pl**, **cl**, **fl**, **gl**, or **sl**.

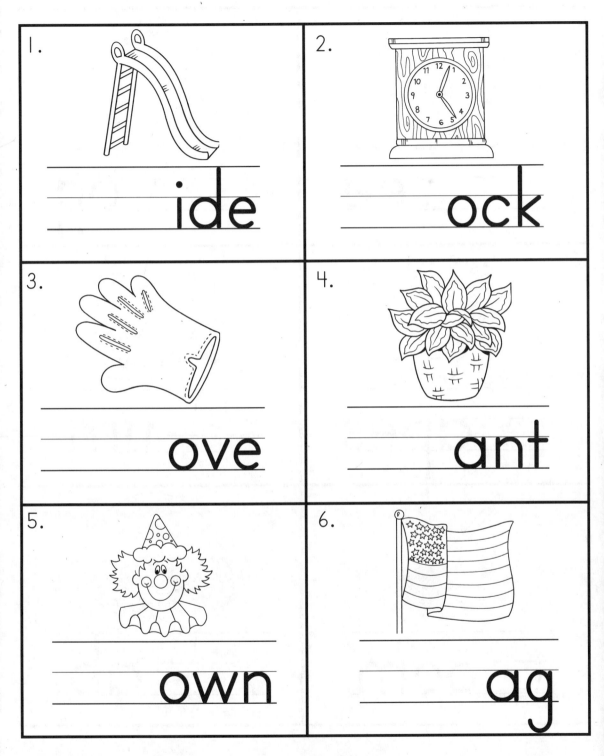

1. _____ide

2. _____ock

3. _____ove

4. _____ant

5. _____own

6. _____ag

Write the missing blend: **br, cr, dr, fr, gr,** or **tr**.

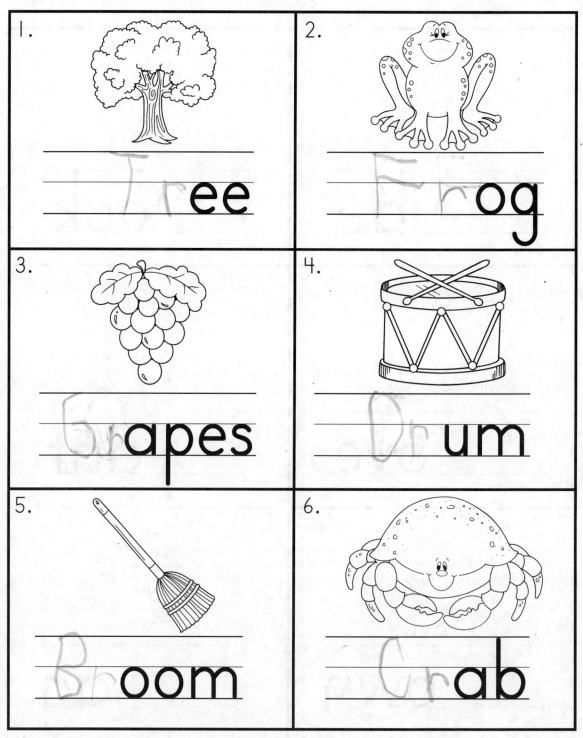

1. Tree

2. Frog

3. Grapes

4. Drum

5. Broom

6. Crab

Curriculum Area: Language Arts **Skills:** Using Blends, Writing

Read the sentences below. If the sentence tells about something that **could** really happen, circle the picture. If it **could not** really happen, place an X on the picture.

1. The girl rode her bike.

2. Horses can fly.

3. The elephant jumps rope.

4. We ate ice cream.

5. We had a picnic.

6. The tree likes to run.

7. The rain fell on the flowers.

8. The boy is fishing.

Curriculum Area: Language Arts   **Skills:** Distinguishing Between Fact and Fantasy

Read the story. Then answer the questions.

Jim went for a walk. He saw birds. He jumped over some rocks. He picked up two orange leaves. It was time for Jim to go home.

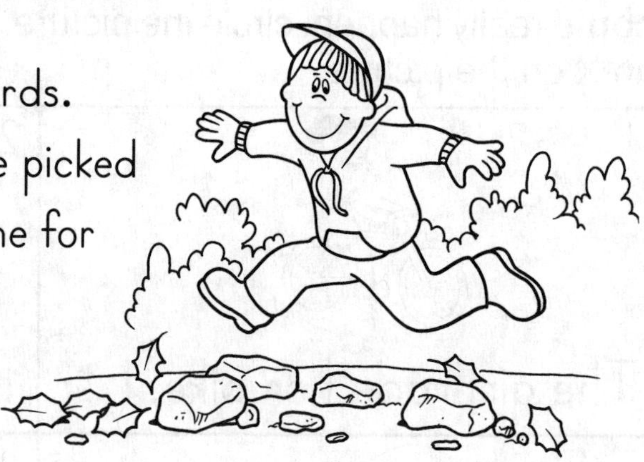

1. What did Jim do?

2. What did Jim see?

3. What did Jim jump over?

4. What did Jim pick up?

Curriculum Area: Language Arts **Skills:** Recalling Facts, Writing

The **cause** is an action. The **effect** is the result of that action.

Draw a line to match each cause with an effect.

Bobby Bunny overslept.

He ate lunch.

Bobby Bunny hopped on a bee.

He was late for school.

Bobby Bunny found some carrots.

He got stung.

Bobby Bunny got a book.

He read a story.

A **contraction** is a combination of two words to make one word.
Example: she is = she's

Write the **contractions** for each set of words.

1. you have _____ ' _____

2. I am _____ ' _____

3. he is _____ ' _____

4. you are _____ ' _____

5. cannot _____ ' _____

6. I will _____ ' _____

A **compound word** is two words put together to make a new word.

play   +   ground   =   playground

Make **compound words** by drawing a line from each word in the left column to the correct word in the right column.

rain	bug
sun	bow
lady	bag
book	shine
snow	walk
side	flake

Look at the pictures and write the compound words on the lines.

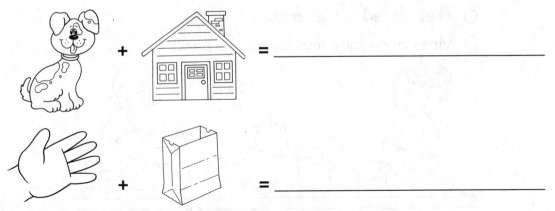

+ _____ = _____

+ _____ = _____

The **main idea** is what the story is mostly about. Read each story and fill in the circle beside the **main idea**.

1. Sue and Pete went to the beach. They went for a swim in the ocean. Then they looked for shells. It was time to go home.

   ○ Sue and Pete went for a swim.
   ○ Sue and Pete went to the beach.
   ○ Sue and Pete looked for shells.

2. Jose and Mark went to the mall. They bought new tennis shoes. For lunch they ate pizza at the food court. Then they went home.

   ○ They bought new tennis shoes.
   ○ Jose and Mark went to the mall.
   ○ Jose and Mark ate pizza.

3. Mary and Jane played on the swings. They went down the slide. They made castles in the sand. Mary and Jane had fun at the park.

   ○ Mary and Jane went down the slide.
   ○ They played in the sand.
   ○ Mary and Jane had fun at the park.

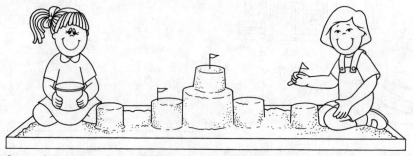

Curriculum Area: Language Arts   **Skills:** Finding the Main Idea

30

Pull-Out Answer Key

Page 1
Each letter should have a corresponding upper or lower case letter next to it.

Page 2
The balloons should be colored according to the directions.

Page 3

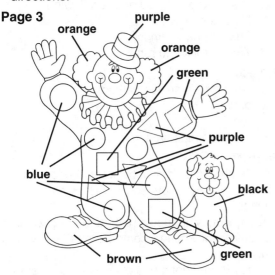

Page 4
The following should be circled:
1. hat, bat
2. bug, rug
3. king, ring
4. pig, wig
5. meat, feet

Page 5
The following should be circled:
1. cat, car
2. door, deer
3. moon, monkey
4. soap, sock
5. hand, house

Page 6
1. bat	2. bed	3. frog
4. soap	5. book	6. fan
7. bus	8. leaf	9. tent

Page 7
A. 3, 1, 2
B. 2, 1, 3
C. 3, 2, 1

Page 8
The following should be circled:
1. dog
2. flower
3. book
4. king
5. shoes

Page 9
The following circles should be filled:
1. shoe	2. car	3. chair
4. star	5. flower	6. clown
7. drum	8. fish	9. mop

Page 10
The following words should be circled:
1. bee	2. boxes	3. socks
4. fly	5. babies	6. bus
7. car	8. glasses	9. mice
10. stars	11. squirrel	12. dishes

Page 11
The title of a story should be written on the writing lines and pictures should be drawn in the boxes.

Page 12
1. Beth James
2. Furry Bunnies
3. Mary Starr

Page 13 and Page 14
Lines should be drawn between these pairs of words:

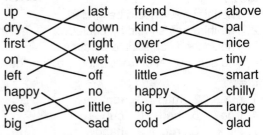

Page 15
A character should be drawn in the space provided and the character's name should be written on the writing lines. There should be one sentence written on the last writing lines.

Page 16
1. apple, boy, cat
2. car, man, up

A

Page 17

Monday, Tuesday, Friday, and Saturday should be written on the lines. The days should be matched to their abbreviations as follows:

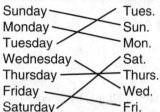

Sunday — Tues.
Monday — Sun.
Tuesday — Mon.
Wednesday — Sat.
Thursday — Thurs.
Friday — Wed.
Saturday — Fri.

Page 18

The following months should be filled in:
May, June, August

Page 19
1. See the dog run.
2. I like to play ball.
3. It is a cloudy day.
4. My friend is named Eve.

Page 20

The following punctuation marks should be circled:
1. period
2. period
3. question mark
4. period
5. period
6. question mark
7. question mark

Page 21
1. The third bee should be circled.
2. The third boy should be circled.
3. The second lion should be circled.
4. The second set of frogs should be circled.

Page 22
1. pig   2. map   3. tent
4. frog   5. bed   6. cup
7. stick   8. rug   9. hand

Page 23
1. slide   2. clock
3. glove   4. plant
5. clown   6. flag

Page 24
1. tree   2. frog
3. grapes   4. drum
5. broom   6. crab

Page 25

The following should be circled:
1. The girl rode her bike.
4. We ate ice cream.
5. We had a picnic.
7. The rain fell on the flowers.
8. The boy is fishing.
An X should be placed on the following:
2. Horses can fly.
3. The elephant jumps rope.
6. The tree likes to run.

Page 26
1. went for a walk (or walked)
2. birds
3. rocks
4. two orange leaves

Page 27

A line should be drawn between the following:
Bobby Bunny overslept. — He was late for school.
Bobby Bunny hopped on a bee. — He got stung.
Bobby Bunny found some carrots. — He ate lunch.
Bobby Bunny got a book. — He read a story.

Page 28
1. you've
2. I'm
3. he's
4. you're
5. can't
6. I'll

Page 29

A line should be drawn between the following:

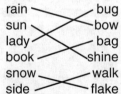

rain — bug
sun — bow
lady — bag
book — shine
snow — walk
side — flake

The following should be written on the lines:
doghouse
handbag

Page 30
1. Sue and Pete went to the beach.
2. Jose and Mark went to the mall.
3. Mary and Jane had fun at the park.

B

Page 31

All of the circles on the page should be colored red. All squares should be colored blue. All triangles should be colored green. All rectangles should be colored purple.

Page 32

The next shape in the pattern should be:
1. triangle
2. sun
3. starfish
4. apple

Page 33

The next shape in the pattern should be:
1. square
2. ball
3. guitar
4. cherries

Page 34

Connect the dots from 1-25 to form a polar bear.

Page 35

Each blank space should be filled in to complete the sequence from 1-50.

Page 36

The missing numerals are as follows:

A. **3**, 4, **5**   B. **18**, 19, **20**
C. **22**, 23, **24**   D. **35**, 36, **37**
E. **40**, 41, 42   F. **77**, 78, **79**
G. **35**, 36, 37   H. **50**, 51, 52
I. **8**, 9, 10   J. **92**, 93, 94
K. **20**, 21, 22   L. **83**, 84, 85
M. 3, **4**, 5   N. 77, **78**, 79
O. 96, **97**, 98   P. 22, **23**, 24
Q. 38, **39**, 40   R. 56, **57**, 58

Page 37

The missing numerals are as follows:
A. 2, 3, **4, 5**, 6, **7, 8**
B. 5, 10, 15, **20, 25**, 30, 35, **40**
C. 2, 4, 6, **8, 10**, 12, **14**, 16
D. 37, 36, **35**, 34, **33, 32**, 31
E. 1, 3, 5, **7, 9**, 11, **13**, 15
F. 10, 20, **30**, 40, **50, 60**, 70

Page 38

1. 9
2. 7
3. 9
4. 5

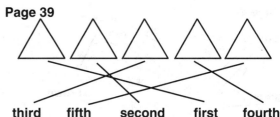

third   fifth   second   first   fourth

The bottom row of triangles should be colored according to the directions.

Page 40

A. 9   B. 7   C. 8
D. 9   E. 6   F. 8
G. 10   H. 6   I. 2
J. 7

Page 41

The answers along the path are as follows:
11, 14, 11, 15, 13

Page 42   6

A. 9   B. 1   C. 9
D. 9   E. 9   F. 9
G. 6   H. 9   I. 6

Page 43

A. 7, 7, 6, 6
B. 8, 5, 4, 10
C. 9, 6, 10, 6
D. 8, 10, 8, 5
E. 10, 9

Page 44

Lines should be drawn as shown:

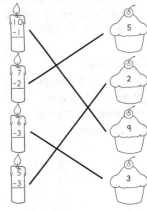

Page 45

A. 1   B. 3   C. 1
D. 2   E. 2   F. 3
G. 2   H. 2   I. 4

C

Page 46

orange · green · brown · red · green · brown · brown · green · blue · blue · orange · red · brown · purple

Page 47
1. 5
2. 3
3. 4
4. 1

Page 48
In the first box, each coin should be matched with its correct name. In the second box, each coin should be matched to its correct amount.
A. 8¢
B. 16¢

Page 49
The matches should be made as following:
    pencil — 1 dime, 2 pennies
    ring — 1 dime, 1 nickel, 1 penny
    apple — 1 quarter, 1 nickel

Page 50
A. 1 nickel, 2 pennies
B. 1 dime, 2 nickels, 2 pennies
C. 1 dime, 1 nickel, 1 penny
D. 1 dime, 1 nickel, 3 pennies
E. 2 nickels, 4 pennies

Page 51
A. 6:00
B. 3:00
C. 12:00
D. 10:00
E. 9:00
F. 5:00
G. 2:00
H. 7:00

Page 52
A. 10:00   B. 6:00   C. 9:00
Each digital clock should be matched to its correct analog clock.

Page 53
For the bear, color 3 spaces. For the lion, color 4 spaces. For the monkey, color 6 spaces. For the elephant, color 1 space.

Page 54
1. 5
2. 3
3. 1
4. 5

Page 55
A. 32
B. 50
C. 75
D. 19
E. 46
F. 64

Page 56
A. $6 + 2 = 8$
   $2 + 6 = 8$
   $8 - 6 = 2$
   $8 - 2 = 6$
B. $7 + 3 = 10$
   $3 + 7 = 10$
   $10 - 7 = 3$
   $10 - 3 = 7$
C. $3 + 2 = 5$
   $2 + 3 = 5$
   $5 - 3 = 2$
   $5 - 2 = 3$
D. $3 + 1 = 4$
   $1 + 3 = 4$
   $4 - 1 = 3$
   $4 - 3 = 1$

Page 57
A. 9
B. 6
C. 9
D. 10
E. 12
F. 8
G. 12
H. 15
I. 6
J. 11
K. 9
L. 12

Page 58
A. 3
B. 8
C. 5
D. 4
E. 1
F. 4
G. 0
H. 1
I. 2
J. 3
K. 2
L. 7
M. 4

Page 59
The shapes should be colored as directed.

Page 60
1. $9 - 3 = 6$
2. $7 - 3 = 4$
3. $5 + 2 = 7$

D

Color the shapes below using the following code.

◯ = red   ☐ = blue   △ = green   ▭ = purple

Decide what should come **next** in the pattern. Fill in the circle beside that picture.

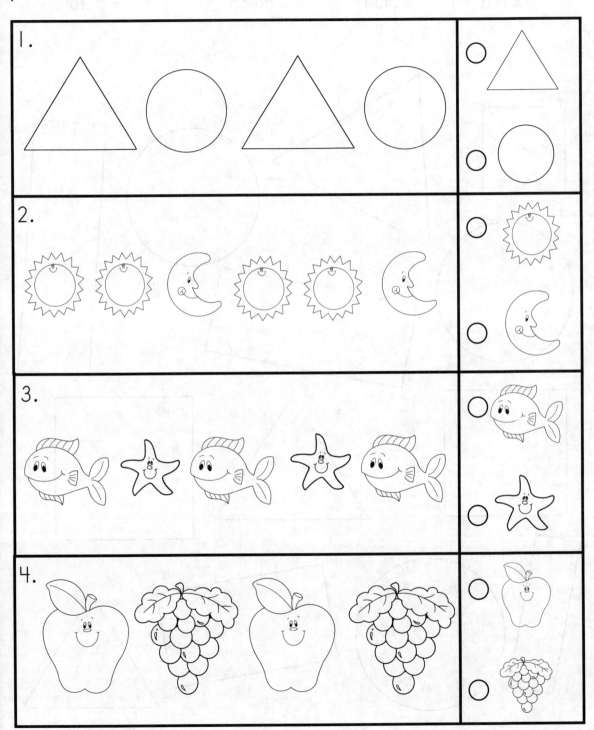

Fill in the circle beside the picture that would come next.

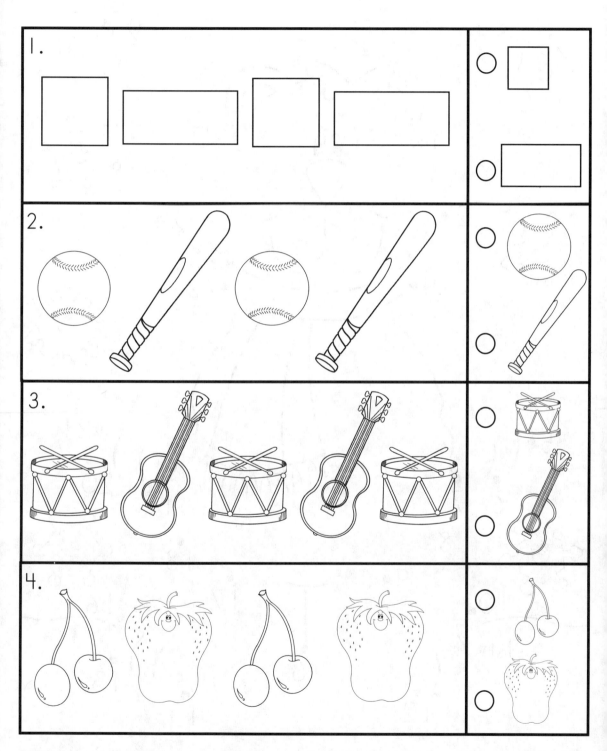

Start at the * and connect the dots to make an animal.

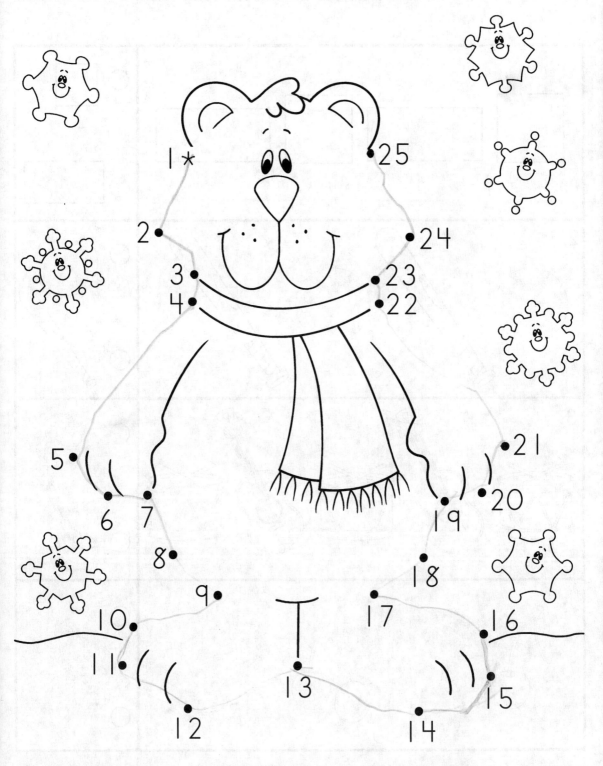

Curriculum Area: Math   **Skills:** Ordering Numerals, Fine Motor Skills

© Carson-Dellosa Publ. CD-6856

Fill in the missing numerals.

1	2	3	4	5
6	7	8	9	10
11	12	13	14	15
16	17	18	19	20
21	22	23	24	25
26	27	28	29	30
31	32	33	34	35
36	37	38	39	40
41	42	43	44	45
46	47	48	49	50

Fill in the missing numerals.

A. _____, 4, _____

B. _____, 19, _____

C. _____, 23, _____

D. _____, 36, _____

E. _____, 41, _____

F. _____, 78, _____

G. _____, 36, 37

H. _____, 51, 52

I. _____, 9, 10

J. _____, 93, 94

K. _____, 21, 22

L. _____, 84, 85

M. 3, _____, 5

N. 77, _____, 79

O. 96, _____, 98

P. 22, _____, 24

Q. 38, _____, 40

R. 56, _____, 58

Fill in the missing numerals. Watch for the pattern in each row.

A. 2, 3, _____, _____, 6, _____, _____

B. 5, 10, 15, _____, _____, 30, 35, _____

C. 2, 4, 6, _____, _____, 12, _____, 16

D. 37, 36, _____, 34, _____, _____, 31

E. 1, 3, 5, _____, _____, 11, _____, 15

F. 10, 20, _____, 40, _____, _____, 70

Study the calendar and answer the questions.

April

Sun.	Mon.	Tues.	Wed.	Thurs.	Fri.	Sat.
	1 ☀	2 ☁	3 🌧	4 ☁	5 🌧	6 💨
7 💨	8 ☀	9 💨	10 ☀	11 ☁	12 🌧	13 ☀
14 ☁	15 💨	16 💨	17 💨	18 ☀	19 ☀	20 🌧
21 🌧	22 ☀	23 💨	24 🌧	25 🌧	26 🌧	27 🌧
28 ☁	29 ☀	30 ☀				

☀ = sunny   🌧 = rainy   💨 = windy   ☁ = cloudy

1. How many sunny days were in April? _____

_____

2. How many windy days were there? _____

_____

3. How many rainy days were there? _____

_____

4. How many cloudy days were there? _____

_____

Curriculum Area: Math   **Skills:** Using Calendar Knowledge, Counting

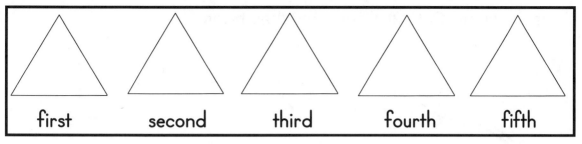

first   second   third   fourth   fifth

Draw a line from each triangle below to the word that shows its place in line. Use the box above to help you.

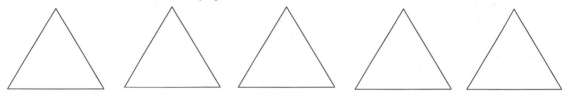

third   fifth   second   first   fourth

Color the following triangles using the directions below.

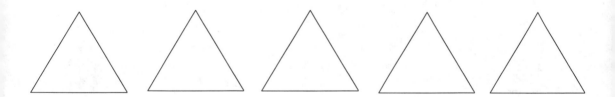

1. Color the first triangle orange.
2. Color the fifth triangle green.
3. Color the third triangle red.
4. Color the fourth triangle yellow.
5. Color the second triangle purple.

Curriculum Area: Math   **Skills:** Sequencing Ordinal Numbers, Following Directions

39

© Carson-Dellosa Publ. CD-6856

Write the sums. Color the bees and their hives.

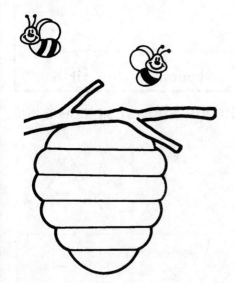

A. 7
   +2
   ___

B. 3
   +4
   ___

C. 6
   +2
   ___

D. 4
   +5
   ___

E. 3
   +3
   ___

F. 7
   +1
   ___

G. 5
   +5
   ___

H. 1
   +5
   ___

I. 1
   +1
   ___

J. 6
   +1
   ___

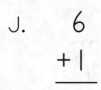

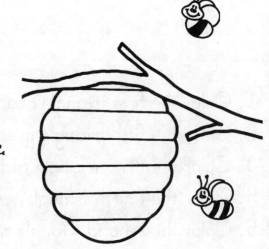

Help Joey find his dog by following the path. Add the problems as you go.

$$\begin{array}{r} 3 \\ +8 \\ \hline \end{array}$$

$$\begin{array}{r} 5 \\ +9 \\ \hline \end{array}$$

$$\begin{array}{r} 9 \\ +2 \\ \hline \end{array}$$

$$\begin{array}{r} 8 \\ +7 \\ \hline \end{array}$$

$$\begin{array}{r} 6 \\ +7 \\ \hline \end{array}$$

Curriculum Area: Math   **Skills:** Adding to 15

Solve the problems. Color all of the apples that have a sum of **9**. How many did you color? _____

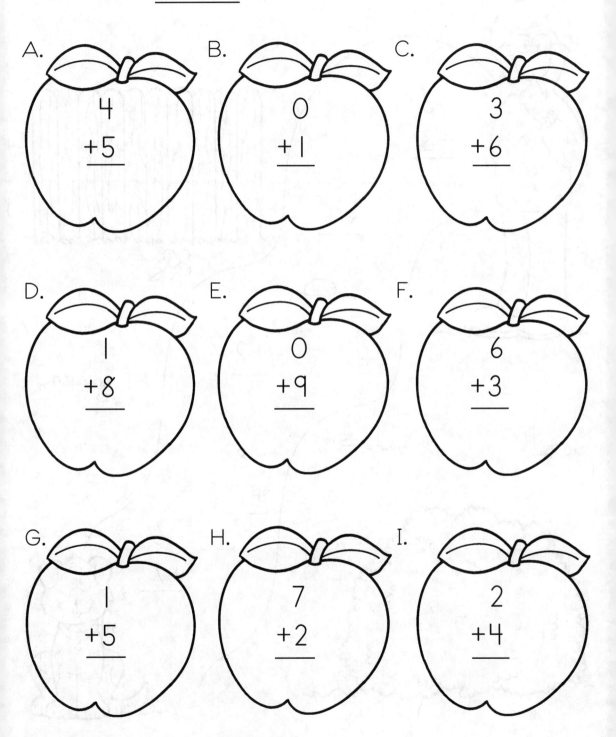

A.
4
+5
___

B.
0
+1
___

C.
3
+6
___

D.
1
+8
___

E.
0
+9
___

F.
6
+3
___

G.
1
+5
___

H.
7
+2
___

I.
2
+4
___

How many addition problems can you solve correctly in two minutes?

A.
$$6 \atop {+\,1}$$
$$3 \atop {+\,4}$$
$$1 \atop {+\,5}$$
$$6 \atop {+\,0}$$

B.
$$7 \atop {+\,1}$$
$$3 \atop {+\,2}$$
$$2 \atop {+\,2}$$
$$5 \atop {+\,5}$$

C.
$$3 \atop {+\,6}$$
$$4 \atop {+\,2}$$
$$4 \atop {+\,6}$$
$$3 \atop {+\,3}$$

D.
$$3 \atop {+\,5}$$
$$10 \atop {+\,0}$$
$$6 \atop {+\,2}$$
$$2 \atop {+\,3}$$

E.
$$9 \atop {+\,1}$$
$$7 \atop {+\,2}$$

Curriculum Area: Math   **Skills:** Adding, Working Under A Time Limit

For each candle, solve the problem and draw a line to the cupcake with the matching answer.

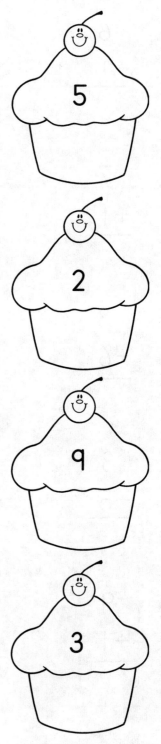

Subtract, then color the flowers.

A.

$$\begin{array}{r} 9 \\ -8 \\ \hline \end{array}$$

B.

$$\begin{array}{r} 6 \\ -3 \\ \hline \end{array}$$

C.

$$\begin{array}{r} 3 \\ -2 \\ \hline \end{array}$$

D.

$$\begin{array}{r} 4 \\ -2 \\ \hline \end{array}$$

E.

$$\begin{array}{r} 8 \\ -6 \\ \hline \end{array}$$

F.

$$\begin{array}{r} 7 \\ -4 \\ \hline \end{array}$$

G.

$$\begin{array}{r} 9 \\ -7 \\ \hline \end{array}$$

H.

$$\begin{array}{r} 7 \\ -5 \\ \hline \end{array}$$

I.

$$\begin{array}{r} 5 \\ -1 \\ \hline \end{array}$$

Curriculum Area: Math

Skills: Subtracting With No Regrouping

45

Add or subtract to solve the problems and then color the picture using the key below:

Key		
4= green	5= orange	6= blue
7= red	8= purple	9= brown

Look at each ruler. Write the length of each object.

A. _____ inches

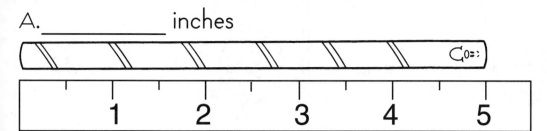

B. _____ inches

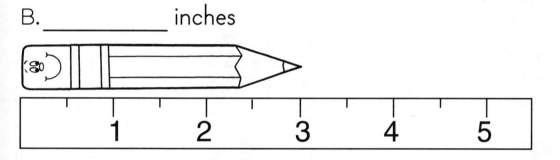

C. _____ inches

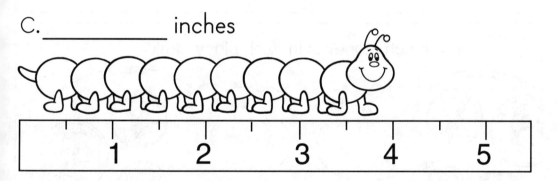

D. _____ inch

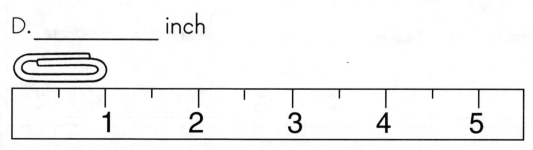

Match the coins to their **names**.

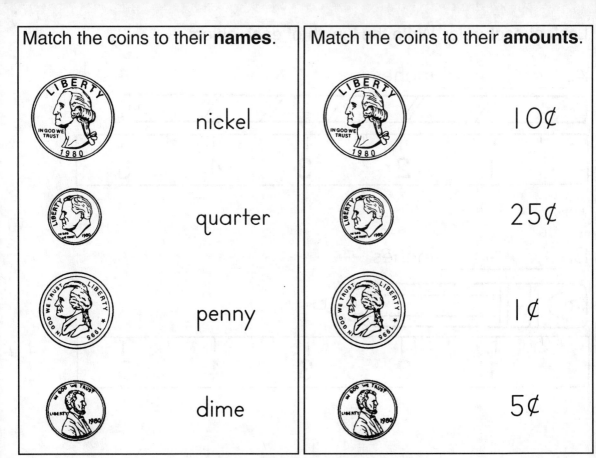

nickel

quarter

penny

dime

Match the coins to their **amounts**.

10¢

25¢

1¢

5¢

How much money is in each piggy bank?

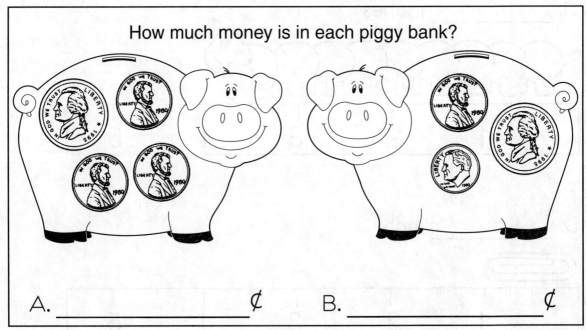

A. _____ ¢   B. _____ ¢

Curriculum Area: Math   **Skills:** Recognizing Coins and Coin Values

Draw a line from each set of coins to the item that sells for that amount of money.

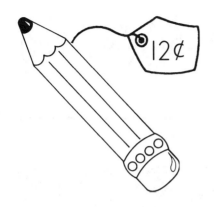 

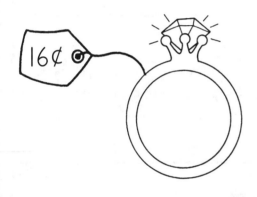 

Circle the coins you need to buy each item.

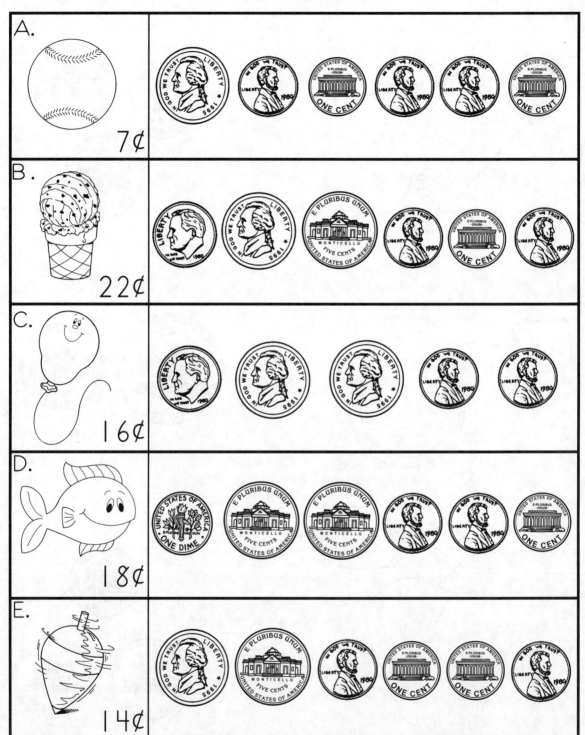

A. 7¢

B. 22¢

C. 16¢

D. 18¢

E. 14¢

Curriculum Area: Math   **Skills:** Recognizing Coins and Coin Values

Write the time you see on each clock.

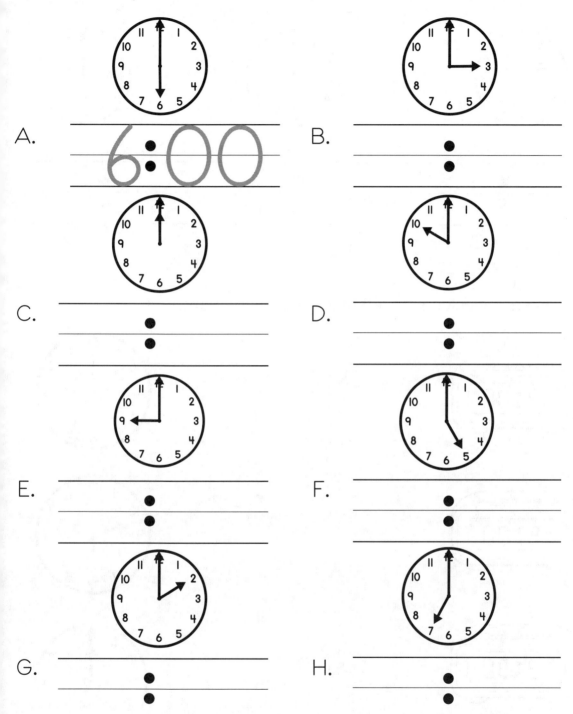

A. 6:00

B.

C.

D.

E.

F.

G.

H.

Write the time shown on each clock.

A.

_____

B.

_____

C.

_____

Match each clock on the left to a clock on the right.

Curriculum Area: Math   **Skills:** Telling Time, Matching

© Carson-Dellosa Publ. CD-6856

At the zoo we saw 3 polar bears, 4 lions, 6 monkeys, and 1 elephant.
Color in the graph to show the animals we saw at the zoo.

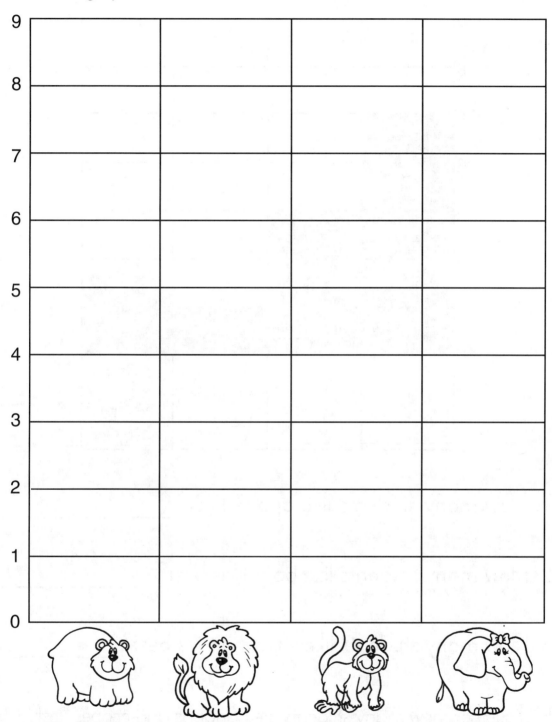

Curriculum Area: Math   **Skills:** Graphing

Another class has given you this graph showing their favorite fruits. Study the graph and answer the questions.

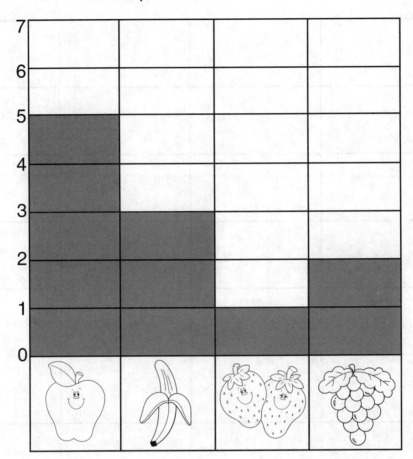

1. How many students like apples best? _____

2. How many students like bananas best? _____

3. How many students like strawberries best? _____

4. Together, how many students like bananas and grapes best?_____

Curriculum Area: Math   **Skills:** Reading Graphs

54

© Carson-Dellosa Publ. CD-6856

On the line below the box, write the numeral each box shows.

tens	ones
3	2

tens	ones
5	0

A. _____

B. _____

tens	ones
7	5

tens	ones
1	9

C. _____

D. _____

tens	ones
4	6

tens	ones
6	4

E. _____

F. _____

Numbers have families, too. Write the missing numerals in each family.

A. family: 6, 2, 8

$6 +$ _____ $= 8$

$2 + 6 =$ _____

$8 -$ _____ $= 2$

$8 - 2 =$ _____

B. family: 10, 7, 3

$7 +$ _____ $= 10$

$3 + 7 =$ _____

$10 - 7 =$ _____

$10 -$ _____ $= 7$

C. family: 5, 3, 2

$3 + 2 =$ _____

$2 +$ _____ $= 5$

$5 - 3 =$ _____

$5 -$ _____ $= 3$

D. family: 4, 3, 1

$3 +$ _____ $= 4$

_____ $+ 3 =$ _____

$4 -$ _____ $= 3$

$4 -$ _____ $= 1$

Curriculum Area: Math   **Skills:** Adding, Subtracting, Working With Number Families

Add.

A.   3   B.   2   C.   6   D.   1
     3   3   0   4
   +3   +1   +3   +5

E.   5   F.   7   G.   2   H.   5
     5   1   4   5
   +2   +0   +6   +5

I.   2   J.   0   K.   1   L.   4
     2   6   5   3
   +2   +5   +3   +5

Curriculum Area: Math   **Skills:** Adding Columns

57

Fill in the missing numerals.

A. $5 - \underline{\hspace{1cm}} = 2$

B. $8 - \underline{\hspace{1cm}} = 0$

C. $6 - \underline{\hspace{1cm}} = 1$

D. $7 - \underline{\hspace{1cm}} = 3$

E. $2 - \underline{\hspace{1cm}} = 1$

F. $8 - \underline{\hspace{1cm}} = 4$ G. $3 - \underline{\hspace{1cm}} = 3$

H. $9 - \underline{\hspace{1cm}} = 8$ I. $7 - \underline{\hspace{1cm}} = 5$

J. $10 - \underline{\hspace{1cm}} = 7$ K. $8 - \underline{\hspace{1cm}} = 6$

L. $9 - \underline{\hspace{1cm}} = 2$ M. $5 - \underline{\hspace{1cm}} = 1$

Follow the directions next to the shapes.

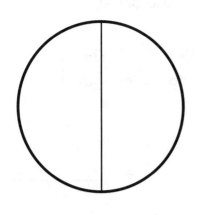

Color $\frac{1}{2}$ of the circle orange.

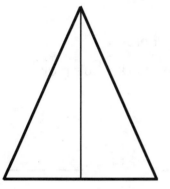

Color $\frac{1}{2}$ of the triangle red.

Color $\frac{1}{2}$ of the triangle yellow.

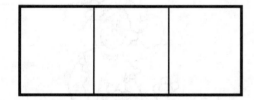

Color $\frac{1}{3}$ of the rectangle green.

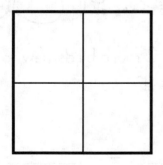

Color $\frac{1}{4}$ of the square blue.

Color $\frac{1}{4}$ of the square purple.

Read the stories and answer the questions. Write a number sentence to show each answer. Don't forget the **+** or **-** in the circle.

1. Together, Steve, and Peter have 9 baseball cards.
    Peter has 3 cards. How many cards does Steve have?

    _____ ◯ _____ = _____

2. Sue and Mary picked 7 flowers all together.
    Mary picked 3 flowers. How many flowers did Sue pick?

    _____ ◯ _____ = _____

3. There were 5 birds on a branch. Then 2 more birds flew to the branch. How many birds were there in all?

    _____ ◯ _____ = _____